Walking Humbly

What does the Lord require of you
but to do justice, and to love kindness,
and to walk humbly   God?

Micah

Walking Humbly

The Holiness of the Poor

By
Father Nicolaie Atitienei,
Mary Marrocco
& Father Roberto Ubertino

St. John the Compassionate Mission

Walking Humbly: The Holiness of the Poor

ISBN 978-0-9959017-2-8
©2017 by St. John the Compassionate Mission

We are grateful to Father George Dion Dragas for permission to use the quotation on page 36.

Published by:
 St. John the Compassionate Mission
 155 Broadview Avenue
 Toronto, Ontario, Canada
 M4M 2E9
 www.stjohnsmission.org

*Dedicated to all
the known and unknown
saints of Toronto.*

ST. LAURENCE OF ROME

Contents

ST. ISADORA OF TABENNA

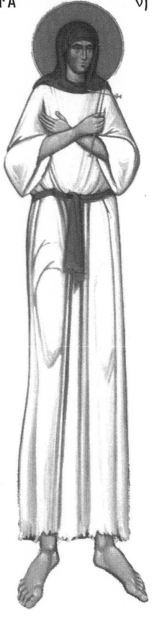

Preface

S t. John the Compassionate Mission was founded in Toronto in 1986. After eight years in a small store-front, it moved to its present location at 155 Broadview Avenue.

The Mission — or "the Church," as it's known on the street — is open seven days a week. Most days start at 5 a.m., with the very marginalized coming for food and rest from a sleepless night. The Mission operates two social enterprises: a non-profit bakery and a thrift store. This allows people to have either a job or acquire the skills to apply for a job. Work is seen as human need, and not just an economic necessity.

Over 4,500 meals have been served at the Mission, but we do not call ourselves a soup kitchen. Through work, sharing food, and different types of help, we offer people a place to belong, a place to feel needed, and a place where we can together learn to become more human.

Like a Pelican in the Wilderness

(Psalm 102:6)

Theological reflections
on the life and circumstances of
St. John the Compassionate Mission
as it enters its
thirty-second year of life

ST. ELIZABETH OF RUSSIA

Introduction

Every week, the *sobor* of St. John the Compassionate Mission in Toronto meets, to reflect and plan the coming week.

These reflections were presented by Father Roberto during one of the meetings.

In these reflections, there is a desire both to encourage and challenge the Mission to live its call to holiness — the holiness of the poor, and not a holiness of fantasy or sugar-coated piety.

Like any other form of holiness in the church, this holiness is both new and ancient. It is creative, and deeply in the tradition.

These teachings try to situate the meaning and life of the Mission as a way of holiness, and not just a form of social service. They represent a calling to discern the taste and smell of the saints of the street, of the fringes of society, and even of the institutional church. They represent our desire to become saints in this place.

The Great Commission
as a Call to Go to the Desert

"Afterward he appeared to the eleven themselves as they sat at table; and he upbraided them for their unbelief and hardness of heart, because they had not believed those who saw him after he had risen. And he said to them, 'Go into all the world and preach the gospel to the whole creation. He who believes and is baptized will be saved; but he who does not believe will be condemned. And these signs will accompany those who believe: in my name they will cast out demons; they will speak in new tongues; they will pick up serpents, and if they drink any deadly thing, it will not hurt them; they will lay their hands on the sick, and they will recover.'

"So then the Lord Jesus, after he had spoken to them, was taken up into heaven, and sat down at the right hand of God. And they went forth and preached everywhere, while the Lord worked with them and confirmed the message by the signs that attended it" (Mark 16:14–20, RSV).

The mission that Jesus gives to the Church in the gospels is followed and accompanied by signs.

Word and sign accompany each other. Demons, snakes, poison and healing are all descriptions of the desert and, today, of our modern cities. As a Mission, we are asked to go into the desert of the city. There we encounter the very realities the Gospel speaks about. It is part of the reality of the Mission that those who come to us not only carry with them the blessing of their poverty and vulnerability, but also at times poison, snakes and demons. For example, when Bob enters the Mission, even before you see him, you can feel the presence of 'another.' Facing the spirit of division and the poison of idle talk, or facing the spirit that unrepentant pedophilia brings, are all part of preaching the Good News. Equally, as well, is the recognizing and the discerning of the grace, wisdom and the holiness of the poor that shine through their brokenness.

The Gospel is challenged, received and revealed through the Mission. Healing comes, but we must also be willing at times to drink the poison and handle the snake. There is no shying away from that. Betrayal of friendship, broken trust and abandonment are the trauma most of the people who come to the Mission have experienced in their lives. At times, we also will experience the same. It is inevitable.

The desert is the place of demons, snakes and deadly danger. The Lord promises that if we are not afraid, if we do not close our door to protect ourselves, but rather go out of our way to welcome and receive the world and all creation (yes even snakes), and excluding no one, if we do that, not only are we not going to be hurt by the real dangers we will face, but healing also will take place. Not only are we not going to get sick, but healing will come from our hands,

Sometimes we are left with very different impressions. For some, Mission means everyone is wonderful. "The poor are holy and grateful." For others, it's all about "how to save people, how to make them Orthodox," how to make them like us. Bring Christ to them. Many religious and socially-minded people who work among the poor act as if there is nothing to learn or receive from the poor. If we have come truly open to receive and learn from the poor, we need to learn to discern the voices of demons and the poison that can kill in us faith, hope and love. We need not to be afraid to name the snakes that slither in, in all forms, all sizes and all shapes. We need *diacresis* (discernment) at all times in the desert, if we are to live the Gospel.

We ourselves need to be prudent as snakes and simple as doves, if we are not to perish in the desert.

The Desert as a Place of Mission

Orthodox mission is a calling to live a reality that most resembles the desert, the place where the prophets cried out, where Jesus was tempted, and where the desert fathers went to search to live. Healing, hope, poison, demons and snakes are all there, all the time, accompanying the Word, confirming the Word or trying to undo the Word. To be faithful to Christ is all that we are asked.

First, to simply look at the Mission as a charity feeding the poor, like a Canadian FOCUS, may help pigeonhole us, but we can't understand ourselves like that, or we will lose our way.

Second, unless we correctly see the reality of the mission, we risk being seriously hurt, through burnout or loss of faith. Cynicism is just a hair-breadth away, and so is acedia.

Third, by wanting to be something else, we fail to respond to the invitation the Lord gives us to live the Great Commission in this place, in these circumstances, and with these people.

What applies to the poor and broken of the world also applies to the 'well-oiled,' and to each of us. The religious professionals and the 'saved' also come, and dare enter the doors of this church. In an authentic way, we are all both evangelizing and being evangelized within the church. This, in great part, is what the Mission is about.

Be warned: the same demons, wolves, poison and snakes can come in many different clothes. Of course, we ourselves can become the carriers of disease to one another. 'The Rule' is a concrete guide in some of the means we can take to be vigilant. We must always refer to the Gospel and the teachings, especially of the desert fathers.

One of the misunderstandings we face vis-à-vis many parishes today is that we are seen as a 'charity.' Why this difficulty in understanding the Mission? I believe it's hard for most people today to have had any other experience of the church outside the average parish and monastery. St. John's Mission also can betray the church by allowing ourselves to become what is easier or more acceptable, such as a well-run 'charity.'

Now, consider that the desert is a place of powerlessness. The reality is that we at the Mission have no power to influence anything, either in the secular world or in the institutional church. I observe that there seems to be a reluctance, at best, to try to ignore that we even exist. So, we inhabit a real desert, as a place where one is vulnerable, and without consequence to anyone. In this sense, for us to be an Orthodox mission, is to try to live the same reality of the poor, who also are without power, and are marginalized, and don't matter to anyone. Such is the place of the desert. Like poverty, this place can be transformed by Love and the Gospel, to a place of great spiritual freedom and joy.

There are many temptations in such a place. The obvious ones are to take the easy way, giving up, bitterness, and cynicism among the few. The other, more subtle, temptation is to find reasons for our lives that show to us and to everyone else what 'good work' we do. Be successful.

Today, in 2017, the call to be in the desert 'poor and naked' has, more than before, a real need, and is of real social significance. Our poverty, our lack of any political or social power, is not 'unfortunate.' In poverty, we can do theology precisely in the way Orthodox theology is at its best. Our lives at the Mission manifest rather than impose the Gospel. Our weakness is a freedom to be simply a witness of what it means to be the Body of Christ. The spirit of the Mission doesn't come from compulsion. We are called in the desert to witness, as a community, that God's purpose in the church isn't running a business, with metrics, marketing and bottom lines.

Society will not protect the work of the Mission or its people. The church institution will not easily protect the life and work of the Mission here in Toronto. Yet what we live seeks to serve and be a place of refuge for both. Only in our desire to love and serve will our "desert become fertile, and our tears water the seeds of the desert flowers that will bloom."[1] It requires patience to be with the young, self-assured atheist, and with the equally sure-of-themselves Orthodox. They will all try to tell us what reality is.

How many Orthodox have told me that "our poor are not deserving or real"? Yet, we need to embrace all with the ascetical silence of the desert, and the willingness to bear the burden of the heat of the day out of love, for no other reason but love itself.[2] This is the heart of the heart of all that truly matters, and only in the desert can one actually be free to live this truth. I am free to love for no other reason than love itself!

In this way, we are most wisely placed by God, not in power, influence or respectability, but in poverty and powerlessness. Only in this way can the church manifest the Kingdom of God. The church today seems not to want to be in the

1. Troparion of ascetics.
2. Cf. Matthew 20:12.

desert. St. John the Compassionate Mission has no choice; we are in it, like it or not.

The Mission, which is intentionally in the desert, witnesses primarily that our essential identity as church lies in the liturgical, spiritual and ascetical service of the world.

We are called to remember that integrity in manifesting the truth is more significant than any desired means of spiritual control. In the desert, the experience of vulnerability, of poverty, is a call to freedom, in the fullest theological sense. As St. Paul says, "My power is made perfect in weakness" (2 Corinthians 12:9).

Toronto is a spiritual desert. This can be hard at times to understand. It is important to really understand that the circumstances in which we find ourselves, in particular ecclesially, are not our doing. They simply are, for a variety of geopolitical-religious reasons, and because of the reality of what Orthodox Christians have, for the most part, chosen to focus and live their lives on. Good or bad, it simply is.

With this particular spiritual desert comes also a feeling of loneliness and aloneness. Is there anyone out there? To live as church in this context is not easy. Yet, as I said before, it represents an opportunity to witness, to both society and the religious establishment, of a fundamental truth of what it means to be the Body of Christ.

The Desert as a Place of Silence

Without Silence, there Is no Presence. Orthodox Mission implies familiarity with Silence.

In Silence, we learn to listen, we learn how to be present to one another. The Desert is the place of silence. Our cities have become places of silence. A modern song sings about the "sound of silence." The silence of the city is the silence that dwells in those who can no longer hear. "There is a sound inside of us all, and in the city we cannot hear it."[1]

This is not the ascetical silence of the saints. Their silence is the source of all words, and these words are about the Word, the Beloved. Silence is about love and communion. The physical silence of the chapel, the silence of our hearts, the silence in the forest, help us also to keep silence beside a person who may not wish to speak to us. Or the silence in front of many life stories and situations where, if you said anything, you would only add to the suffering.

Silence helps us to live the most important work of the Mission: being truly present, in communion with each person we encounter. Silence

---

1. Spoken by a youth from Covenant House in Toronto, about his visit to the rural St. Mary of Egypt Refuge.

helps us to hear the music all around us, for "the music is not in the notes but in the the silence between them."[2]

It is the ascetical silence of John the Baptist that allows him to become smaller, so that Jesus can be more visible. Later, it is the silence in his prison that allows Jesus' preaching and ministry to grow. It's the silence of the angels' song that St. Maximus describes: "silence, rich in speech and tone."

Silence is the willingness to live out of poverty, out of not having, out of not knowing, and sharing rather what we are. Many good things can come out of learning to hold another person in this ascetical silence, a heart that knows when to wait in silence, and when to speak. The difficulty with silence is that in our age of blogs, web sites, etc., to be silent means to have nothing to say. Our world sees silence as not having, not being — it is being poor. Often, the truly poor people will appear to us as a silent type. How many tell me they just want to be left alone, feeling that no one would listen to them anyway? Yet, these silent ones that sit at our table hold an infinite ocean, of darkness and of light. In front of another, we don't want to appear poor, ignorant or ineffectual, and much of our talking is only about that.

There is really very rare communication, because without silence no one hears.

2. Attributed to composer Claude Debussy.

Orthodox Mission is lived out in the context of a social silence that grows like a cancer. Nonetheless, by freely accepting this apparent poverty, we live this desire to be really present to God, to ourselves and to others. Love demands silence in the presence of the Beloved, so that it can find the words that truly speak to the heart. The ascetical silence of the saints is about learning to speak the language of the heart, a language that we lost over time since leaving paradise. "Civilization is the loss of the heart" (Bishop Hierotheos).

At the Mission, if you don't learn this language, the language of the heart, you will never be able to hear and speak to another.

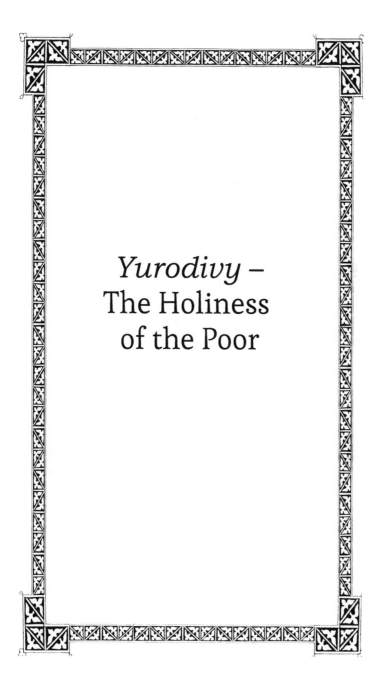

Yurodivy –
The Holiness
of the Poor

ST. ЖЕПIA   FOOL ЃOЃ ChЃISТ

W hat is the way of holiness for the Mission? It must be one that is the same for both those who come to live and serve, and for those who walk through its doors and become part of this community.

I think this is what I have been trying to answer for years, when I ask, "What is Orthodox mission?" An Orthodox Mission can't just be a Salvation Army with icons...or even a form of the Catholic Worker, with bells and smells...

So then, what is Orthodox mission?

In part, I believe this is answered in the article on the Anchorites we read, and by the reflections under the chapter title, "Like a Pelican in the Wilderness."

There is another aspect, more personal, which involves Holiness. What is the holiness of the poor?

I believe an important door opens for us when we see that the type of holiness that best matches our concrete daily reality is found in the holy fools (*yurodivy* — literally, 'the odd ones').

Let me try to explain. I will take some of my inspiration from Christos Yannaras, but only in as much as it actually is reflected by our experience at the Mission.

Let us begin by saying the obvious. The Gospel, in many ways, has been 'taken hostage' by the consequence of the fall of Adam. The consequence of the fall imprisons us in our egocentric, self-imposed alienation. The fall thus equates sin with individual guilt. Repentance (*metanoia*) then becomes individual improvement and salvation, and with being socially useful and following socially-acceptable norms. In the life of the Church, we have examples and places where we see this overturning and rejection of individual morality. Here is one.

St. Zoticus' city of lepers is a good example of this Gospel foolishness, one that even goes against God's representative on earth, the Holy Emperor, by breaking the law and threatening civil order!

This story later is sweetened, and becomes only a story of individual moral generosity and the practice of an individual vocation, now a safe and acceptable virtue of a harmless saint. No one asks the question, but if this is all he is about, then why did St. Zoticus end up being murdered by a Christian emperor?

I believe we can find an answer to the question St. Zoticus raises by looking to the so-called *yurodivy*, the 'fools for Christ.'

"We are fools for Christ" (1 Corinthians 4:10), St. Paul being the first of them!

The *yurodivy* intentionally break the expectations of society, of what normally constitutes virtue and reward, to embrace the way of the Gospel.

To be a real *yurodivy*, one does not choose what leads us to this path, but rather it is a path God puts us on. St. Xenia did not start her marriage wanting to be a fool for Christ. The violent death of her husband that shattered all her dreams and took away her husband led her to this path. Mother Maria did not choose to have two divorces and end up in a concentration camp. At times, there are real psychological wounds that make certain people unable to be 'normal.' These are the people God can choose to show us the freedom of the Gospel.

Life events have led you here in this Mission, not your plans of wanting to be virtuous or charitable. We often are drawn to stay at the Mission not because of the sense of our great gifts and talents, but out of the experience of our own brokenness: mental breakdown, divorce, loss of work, loneliness, fitting nowhere, depression. All are doors that have led many to come and stay here. It can also be the reason why people leave. Having your illusions stripped away can also be a place of temptation.

This is the first necessary ingredient in discerning this type of holiness as authentic in us. God chose this path for us.

The second point to consider is realizing that you are the same as the people you came to 'help.' Yes, I am no different than Rob or Kevin, no different than all the people who come and sit down at the 'table of the poor' in this church.

In admitting this, something deeper happens in my soul. I refuse to see myself as an individual, separate, locked in my auto-sufficiency. I repent of the sin of Adam. I enter into the Gospel call of *metanoia*. I step out of the demonic illusion and thoughts that say to my soul, "*I need no one, I touch no one and no one touches me, I am a rock...a holy rock, an island unto myself. An island of virtue, piety and virtue, not like the rest of the people I serve.*" In refusing this logismos, I choose to live the common nature that we all share. I live the repentance of the publican.

This leads me to desire a personal relationship with those who are damned, in a spirit of repentance and communion.

In this way, God calls the fools to overcome the fragmentation of our nature caused by sin, changing sin, even my personal failings, and into a humble, non-demanding acceptance of others.

The third aspect of this way of holiness is in the complete abandonment of the ego. This means I take the risk of being seen as vulnerable, and as sinful. In this way, we win the confidence and trust of the poor, and those outside the structures of power.

The fourth element of being a fool for Christ is the real sense that what the poor suffer, including the suffering caused by sin in their lives, does cleanse, and that many, because of this suffering, "shine like the sun." Thus, I desire to be close to them (cf. Daniel 12:3 and Matthew 13:43).

The fifth consequence of this way of holiness is that we witness (*martyria*) that to be in Christ, one must accept the common fall and sin. The goal of the Christian life is not respectability or virtue, and thus the particular martyrdom of this way of life. We will be of no value or use, even in the eyes of many people in the church; we will be seen as useless. The reality that the *yurodivys* witness is in this, that even our religious and social categories can keep us locked in our private, comfortable hells, separated from God and from each other.

"The way of the fools for Christ, is a way of witnessing by our life, the gospel truth that it is enough for a person to humbly accept their own sin and fall, without making it different from the sin and fall of the rest of mankind, trusting in the love of Christ which transfigures this acceptance into personal nearness and communion, into a life of incorruption and immortality." (Yannaras)

The Jesus Prayer is the prayer of the poor, of the fool for Christ: "Lord Jesus Christ, have mercy on me *the* sinner." The sinner that one prays for is not the individual self, but the ecclesial man who has become the Adam. The heart of the fool for Christ has been broken by life, and through grace becomes open to all.

As with so many things, even this way of Holiness (that in particular belongs to the poor and the marginalized) has been made to become part of an individualistic understanding of the Gospel, reserved for an elite. Fools for Christ become respectable, canonical, acceptable...the Kremlin's church is dedicated to St. Basil, Fool for Christ!!! Nonetheless, as Yannaras says, "it is the calling of every member of the church."

At the Mission, there is an opportunity to live some of the creativity of such Gospel foolishness, in a refreshing way.

I believe it gives to us a way to live authentically among the poor. This does not mean becoming holy by using the poor, but becoming holy with the poor.

In this way, they truly become our teachers and masters, something we discover every day in a new and wonderful way, even though it's not always easy or without much suffering.

I believe that it is in the way of the *yurodivy* that we find how to live Orthodox mission today in Toronto. Light comes through the cracks, as Leonard Cohen's song 'Anthem' has it. I pray that this is the start of such a reflection on our life at the Mission.

"O God, send us fools,
who offer themselves wholly,
who let go,
 who love without words,
who give themselves truly and to the end.
We need fools,
the unreasonable,
the passionate,
who can leap into insecurity,
into the ever yawning gulf of poverty.
We need fools for now,
enchanted by the simple life,
loving peace,
cleansed of compromise,
firm against betrayal,
heedless of their own lives,
ready to undertake anything,
or go anywhere:
at the same time obedient,
spontaneous and decided,
gentle and strong.
O God, send us fools."

(This prayer, by Father Louis-Joseph Lebret, was put to music and sung every night throughout the world by the Pain de Vie community, with which the Mission was for many years affiliated.)

The Parish
of the Poor

ST. PERPETUA

Each historical time has its own challenges. The Church does not exist in a vacuum, or in historical 'suspended animation.' It needs to be incarnated. In the life of the Church, monasteries and parishes have been the two places where most people experience what Salvation looks like, 'in real time.' The monasteries and parishes incarnate the truth of the Gospel for each generation.

St. John the Compassionate Mission is not trying to be innovative, but rather traditional, and returning to the original roots of what a parish life is simply meant to be. We don't try to be a monastery, even though there are aspects of parish life that are similar, like hospitality.

That most church buildings on our continent today are closed during the work week, and for the most part serve only a specific group of people, does not mean that the present manifestation of parish life has always been the norm. The present 'normal parish,' even with the best of liturgical performances, is not 'traditional.' It is an innovation to see the church as uniquely a 'worship center' for Sundays and feast days.

Nonetheless, this reflection is not about trying to correct anyone; we don't try to teach anyone anything. We are moved to reflect, and to seek to live out, the full potential of parish life, both on Broadview Avenue and Markham Road. What we are to reflect on is what parish life can look like, from the perspective of our own limited experience, and in the historical context in which we find ourselves. We must start from the understanding that the Church is not just in the heart of the world, but that the Church is the heart of the world. Therefore, a parish is not made up just of its 'membership' (however we define this), but includes everyone who lives around it, and who come to its doors for a variety of reasons. There are no outsiders for us in the parish. Therefore, the lives and concerns of all those around us belong to us, and are part of our concerns and care.

We need some reflection on this question, on who is in the Church, from dogmatic and pastoral points of view. In present-day Russia, for example, and as in most historical Orthodox nations, the Church claims a large part of the population: seventy-five percent Orthodox, yet only five percent of those regularly attend church. Even with only five percent of membership attending, the Church still acts and understands itself as being the church of the people. It seeks to minister to all in society, and to influence society. It is true that this is based on the ethnic and historical origins of this particular church. However, do not being human and attending church, for whatever everyday reason (like our Mission's 'breakfast people'), constitute being in the embrace of the Church? What about those who grew up with no religious formation? Are they not part of the Church also?

In other words, is not the Incarnation the basis for our understanding of where the boundaries of the Church are?

At compline, for example, I believe that when we pray for those who are absent, we are praying for all the people who through the day have come to the Mission, but for whatever reason are absent at that moment. For those who are absent for worthy reasons from the liturgy, could they not also include all those whom we pray for? Might this not also include those possessed by unclean spirits; those in jail; those in all kinds of tribulations, trials and trauma; those with mental and physical brokenness; and those with addiction?

As with monasteries, parishes in pagan lands are dynamic engines of renewal of people's lives (such as Ora et Labora), and even of evangelization of whole nations. The traditional model of evangelization that we see in the early Church, for example, with St. Eusebius of Vercelli (a strong supporter of the council of Nicaea), and by whom my ancestors claim to have been directly evangelized, was known for his deep compassion for the people around him. He wanted the Church to live in community, which included a strong commitment to communal poverty, with faithful men and women living together. From this 'center of parish life,' or 'mother church,' as it was called, northwestern Italy was evangelized. One of the earliest translations of the New Testament, dating from before Jerome's Vulgate, was done under Eusebius' authority in his effort to evangelize the local people.[1] He did this because he really cared for the people to whom he brought the Gospel.

I use this example so as not to repeat the same Basilian model of the famous 'Basiliad' (and those of other Eastern fathers), giving the false impression that this was the only such attempt in the life of the Church. It was a universal practice that in every diocese the Church would also have Houses of Hospitality. These were under the direct supervision or responsibility of the Bishop, who presided at the Eucharist. There was even a canon

---

1. *Codex Vercellensis* and *Vita Antica.*

(now forgotten) of the council of Nicaea about this very practice.

The parish is the place where the Eucharist is served, offering the Eucharist "Τὰ σὰ ἐκ τῶν σῶν σοὶ προσφέρομεν κατὰ πάντα καὶ διὰ πάντα" ("for all and for the sake of all"). Therefore, and equally, those who through union with Christ in communion receive the Eucharist live out their lives "for all and for the sake of all": "Καὶ πάντων καὶ πασῶν" ("for each and every one").

It is not about keeping our doors open, to "those yet to be Orthodox." It is about being the Ark of Salvation for all, receiving each person — and especially the poor and marginalized — as another, as vicars of Christ. It was the unique and exclusive practice of the historical Church to care for all, and not just its members, that separated it from other contemporary charities. This was a revolutionary practice that would subvert the natural order of society, which was itself believed to have been established by the very gods.

Where was this new order most visible? It was visible in the Eucharist, where now even a slave could be the presider. In fact, it is this practice of universal love that was most in conflict with Roman society, values and civil religion. That is why Christians were called the first atheists.

Today, and it seems in paradox, the same so-called historical Church lives the opposite. In the minds of the average member of the clergy or the average person, it is secular society that is seen as being concerned for all, with the Church concerned only for itself. Nonetheless, the Eucharist calls us to receive and reach out to each person. But this welcome does not treat people as "ministry cases," but as true Brothers and Sisters on the journey, and on the walk toward the Kingdom. We are called to understand the heart of the human being, as made for God, regardless of where she or he is in their journey toward the Kingdom.

We can do this because the parish is primarily the place where the Eucharist is offered, and where those who offer it live their lives as living sacrifice, seeking also to become broken bread, for the life and salvation of all. Therefore, it is important that the celebration of the liturgy not be simply one of the many devotions of our life, another of the "five" ascetical practices of self-improvement, but rather the center, the beginning and end of all we do, are and want to become.

It is also necessary that we spend time in the chapel praying alone or in community, and in silence, prolonging the communion we have received, and offering our time, body and mind to Jesus, in a direct and simple way. This is also where we learn to listen and welcome each other and others, in the liturgy and after the liturgy. Without this silence, the liturgy after the liturgy can become just social work.

This sense that "the work" of the Church is to be the incarnation of the body of Christ cannot happen through us, unless we are inebriated by the fire of the Holy Spirit, the fire that we receive in Communion. Equally in us, there must be a burning desire to let this fire burn in our whole being and through us, with all we welcome in the parish. This fire in us must burn: this cannot be stressed enough.

There is also a particular ascetical life that is proper to the parish life, and that is different from the life lived by those who are in monasteries. The difference is in the expression, but not in the essence or in its intensity.

Communion is received not based on merit, but based on whether one is willing to try to live with God's help, with what one has received, and to become what we receive in communion. "Broken and shared, like this bread offered for all in all and for the sake of all": "Καὶ πάντων καὶ πασῶν" ("for each and every one").

The ascetism of the liturgy is to be vigilant, and we are not to make worship a 'form,' an end in itself. For the esthetical, music and beauty are important, but when they are separated from a desire to truly enlarge our hearts, and exclude no one from them, they become another form of idolatry. The aim of the ascetical life for those in the parish, as for those who live in monasteries, is exactly the same. This end, 'telion,' is universal love: a love that is boundless, and that excludes no one. Apathia is not lack of sensitivity, but rather is a love that is not conditioned either by suffering or by pleasure. The end, the telion, is to exist as Christ, who exists in agony in the poor man, and will until the consummation of time.[2]

This universal love (to repeat until we get it) is based on the fact that the Liturgy is offered for ALL: "Τὰ σὰ ἐκ τῶν σῶν σοὶ προσφέρομεν κατὰ πάντα καὶ διὰ πάντα."

---

2. St. Maximus the Confessor and the Church Mystagogy: "In this Mystagogy, Saint Maximus presents us above all with the total mystery of the Church, which embraces all reality in its totality and its parts, and gives it an eternal significance. He is able to do this by employing the Greek Patristic ontological category of the eikon. Thus, the Church is presented as a reality, which does not stand over or against the world but alongside, with and for the world, viz. as a reality, which reveals its proper function. Indeed the Church is the proper eikon of the world. She is the world seen in another perspective which is more human, and which is imbued with a divine quality of being and manner of existence. Saint Maximus

The exclusion of some from Communion is part of the discipline of the Church, but its intention is to reconcile, and not to push away forever the sinners. Even here, some who do not receive communion may be closer to Christ than those of us who do. We need canons to regulate the life of the visible Church, but we are in illusion (fantasia) if we think that they limit the work of the Spirit or completely define the Church. Father Nicolas Afanassieff has written well on the limits of Canon Law in Church life.[3] The present obsession with quoting the Pedalion seems to replace the fire of the Gospels and limit the understanding of the reality of the Church. It seems as if we all woke up one morning, specialists in Church canons!

Ascetical life, when in reference to the Eucharist, is understood as the way by which we can participate in God's kenotic love, and in the measure we can, given our sinfulness. Sinfulness is not about breaking rules, but about limiting our capa-

---

leads us to see the great mystery of the Church in the specific and realistic eikons which constitute our total everyday experience, and which, far from opposing one another, help distribute the light of God's glory and truth from the outer galaxies of heaven to the innermost sanctum of the soul, the human mind. In this perspective the Church is a manner of existence, which transforms all creaturely existence in its totality and in its parts without leaving anything outside." [Father George Dion Dragas, "Church in St. Maximus's Mystagogy: The Problem and the Orthodox Perspective," *Theologia* (Athens), vol. 56:2 (1985): 385–403.]

3. *L'Église du Saint Esprit*, P. Nicolas Afanassieff.

city to become the Eucharist. As a poor person in Scarborough reminded me, "Sin is what gets in the way of the way of Love." We touch the body of Christ in Communion, and we touch the Body of Christ in welcoming the poor person. How Christ is present in each person is not up to speculation, but rather we are to receive the body of Christ in faith and the fear of God with love: "Μετὰ φόβου Θεοῦ, πίστεως καὶ ἀγάπης προσέλθετε."

The poor will concretely help the parish be missionaries by their very presence, and they will keep the parish from being closed upon itself. If the poor are truly part of the parish, we won't need to find ways to reach out. They will challenge us in our understanding of the faith, and in the importance of the liturgy and all its dimensions. They will teach us that if Christ is not risen, than we know despair only.

The squabbles over jurisdictions, minute canons and rules take on a very different flavor in the context of real lives, with real problems and real suffering. The parish gives flavor and color to the lives of all those around her, and to those who come to her. You are the light of the world and the salt of the earth. The parish of the poor is about giving flavor to daily life, and not about making the whole world a pile of salt. It is about being a leaven, and making bread so people can eat, but without making everything into leaven.

Births, marriages, deaths, divorces, recent releases from jail, losses, homelessness, not having a family, being single: all sorts of human situations that today are so widely spread, find in the parish a place of welcome. In the parish, there is the offer and possibility of healing, or, at least, a physical place of no despair, and a place of hope.

The parish is a place of non-demanding welcome, as it was for Joe the other day, when he was starting to have the 'shakes' because he had not had a drink since the morning. He returned shortly after speaking to us, and with tears in his eyes he asked if I could give him a hug. He wept in my arms. I had not met Joe before. His hands, black from never washing, were trembling, and his face was deeply carved out by the years. Who had told him that this was a safe place where he, the unrepentant alcoholic, could finally break down and cry in the arms not of a man but of the Merciful Father? Was it not Christ who drew this man into the church that afternoon? All we had to do was open our arms to him. This was without saying a word, and without videos or instructional theological courses. We need to be there, so Christ can welcome them. That is all that it is asked of us.

This is why I have this real sense and certainty that when we bring the Eucharist in a place that is abandoned, Christ radiates through us, even in our defective ways and with all our limitations. When we celebrate the Liturgy, the Church comes to be in the midst of the people. The adventure is then in discovering the many ways this is true. Like the gospel says, "Wherever the corpse is, there the vultures will gather" (Matthew 24:28). People know where there is food, where to find bread, and where there is the water for their thirst. In the Eucharist present among us, the parish has the bread and the water people seek. Everything in the parish becomes Eucharistic. The table where we serve the meals, the door we open to welcome, the cup of friendship (the coffee mug), the listening, the resources we share, all come from the blessing of the Eucharist. We believe that the celebration of the Eucharist changes how people experience their lives. We can do this simply and humbly by letting Joe, for example, cry on our shoulders. We can also do this by sharing the cup of friendship with some lost newcomers just out of jail.

A lot of our work is not in what we say, but how we look at people. Words but also looks have a powerful effect on people and the so-called "outcomes." Today we can't say much any more to people. Too much is being said, and too many words are uttered, so that the Word has lost its power to convince.

What we can still do is change how we look at a person. We can look at a person with hope, in love and with faith, or we can be cynical and fatalistic. Harm reduction, for example, is a form of fatalism, masked under pseudo-compassion. Assisted suicide is another collective way to affirm that some people's lives are really not worth living. The list is long. The asceticism of parish life includes never looking at anyone with lust. In other words, it is to look at a person without only our personal interest or agenda at heart.

Cynicism, dismissal, fatalism and despair of the other are ways of looking at another with lust and not purity of heart. This warfare is at times very intense, because the temptations are real. You can only talk to the same drug addict high on coke for so many times. You can only bury people who overdosed so many times, and you can only bear the self-righteousness of the religious professionals for so long.

Only in the ascetical struggle to have a pure heart can we persevere to seek, to see correctly, and to see that in doing this it is promised that we will see God. The gospel assures that those with purity of heart will see God. They will see God, where others see only despair, ugliness, death, and lack of any value. We must struggle in prayer and fasting, for this purity of vision of the heart. Orthodoxy is not just about having the truth, but being able to see God, truly.

Fasting and prayer are of course very powerful means, but the test of the authenticity of our prayer and fasting is in how well we see the poor and the things around us. Do we see God, or just our own frustrations, judgments and self-interests. Is our heart so enlarged that it can hold hope for all? Without this purity of heart and vision of God, we will grow tired and become a simple institution that serves itself. We will not be the parish that incarnates the Eucharist through its daily life. The parish is then the body of God in a particular place, among "these people." This is the Eucharist that is the fulfillment of the world.

The parish priest is at the heart of this community. He speaks the words of Christ and does the acts of Christ. He offers the sacrifice and gives it to us, so we may become it. Everyone in the parish, who with the priest offer the Eucharist, is called to live out this movement of offering. We must encourage the many charisms that are present in the parish, that manifest the richness of this life, and that are offered to the world. All who in some way are part of the parish, even if not as communicants, by virtue of their humanity share a desire to even just take refuge in the parish, as part of the Church.

They do carry the "mystery" (*mysterium tremendum*) within them, especially the poor and the vulnerable. We must not see them as "not yet Orthodox," for really only God knows who is Orthodox and who is not, as Blessed Augustine reminded people in his city many centuries ago.

Maybe it is me and not Joe who is "not yet Orthodox."

People today no longer believe in or have ever known unconditional love. Even our desire to want to change another, as a starter in our conversation, will do damage to their heart, and will smell like everything else in the world. Only God is so rich in Mercy that he can love us, and welcome each of us with no demands. We are to witness to this Apathia, this love, not because of gain, or an agenda, or even a holy agenda, but simply because first of all there is Love.

Christ loves Joe, so I can just love him as he is. This often means suffering with, loving, and letting the suffering in! I need to hold in my heart this truth, especially if Joe has forgotten it or never known it. What an immense privilege this is! "Καὶ πάντων καὶ πασῶν" ("for each and every one").

Our parish will renew itself each day through the Eucharist, lived out concretely in the service of all, but especially the poor, by a witness of a love that is utterly freeing, a love that has seized us and that burns ever more concretely, deeply in our hearts.

"Τὰ σὰ ἐκ τῶν σῶν σοὶ προσφέρομεν κατὰ πάντα καὶ διὰ πάντα."

Flowers
From
the
Hedges

ST.   SARAH

Introduction

J ohn Moschus wrote the famous *Pratum Spir-ituale* (translated as 'The Spiritual Meadow'), a collection of stories of early ascetics. For the first time, these men and women were presented as flowers in the spiritual garden, a garden of the church in the desert.

The Mission has collected a series of flowers on the very edge of this spiritual meadow...the flowers that Jesus in Luke 14:23 speaks about: "Go out to the highways and hedges, and compel people to come in, that my house may be filled." The city is this new desert, inhospitable and formidable, where we find people living on the hedge, who don't fit in any system or category, wild men and women, yet walking humbly the way of holiness, at times even unaware of it themselves. The church gathers such flowers from the hedges and gives glory to God.

This is holiness on the hedge, yet still, "He rests among these saints."

(All the stories in this chapter describe real lives, but some use pseudonyms.)

1. Peter

Peter Stire came to the Mission on Blake Street, brought by a couple he had met at the Salvation Army downtown.

Peter lived both the Blake Street and Broadview realities of St. John the Compassionate Mission. He decided to ask for Baptism during a retreat weekend the Mission held at Collingwood. This was a surprise for me, to receive from Peter such a request, since he would mostly yawn during my talks. His mouth would open up as big as a horse and one time, exasperated, I put a shoe in it! The day Peter stepped into the baptismal font, he later said, it was so deep that he did not think his feet would ever touch the bottom.

His simplicity, and his self-effacing disposition, were disarming. Therefore, he got away with his favorite routine of preaching to the bus drivers about his new love, Jesus Christ. He tried giving up smoking: he had left his cigarettes before he was baptized at the altar call during a 'Sally Ann' revival meeting. After his baptism, he eventually took his pack back. I will never forget his look of dismay when, one day as he was smoking outside the front of the Mission, another, not-so-gentle

preacher approached Peter out of the blue, and promised him eternal damnation because since he was a smoker, he obviously did not know the Lord.

There are enough stories about Peter that easily a book could be written, and I plan to do so. He had a very simple, childlike faith, and I have personally witnessed how his prayer could work miracles. Like the day when he stopped the rain, just long enough for us to bless the sea.

Peter's holiness shone, along with his human poverty and brokenness. I have a beautiful picture of him against the sun, shining and smiling at the camera. This picture for me is an icon of what the Lord speaks about in the Gospel, when he says that in the kingdom, we will all shine like the sun.

Peter never read or studied, but he could come up with deep theological insights, especially about the Mother of God. He loved her icon in our chapel, and to this day one can see how the gold of her robe has been worn out by his tender kisses.

My last visit with Peter before he died was in the nursing home, where he had been locked in the ward for mentally deranged seniors. Apparently, he had become aggressive because they told him he could not smoke. During the visit, he went to confession. His last words to me as I was leaving were, "Father, I have one great sadness. I have never been able to have tears for my many, many, many sins."

Shortly after his death, I had a dream where Peter came and helped me carry a cross up a hill. At his funeral, there were Roman Catholics of both rites, Orthodox, people from the Salvation Army, and unbelievers of all sorts — and even Québécois who had come to be there for him.

To this day, I feel that Peter works miracles among us, in a humble and quiet way. How else could you explain that the Mission is still open?

His life really touched everyone he met. It helped me to understand how real holiness can exist alongside our own brokenness and poverty. In fact, it is those who are poor that best show us what holiness is. "Blessed are they who know that they are poor, for theirs is the kingdom of heaven."

Yet, Peter's life took its full potential, and meaning, and place in the Kingdom of Heaven because God drew him into the Church, and into the Church his life blossomed to its full potential, and eventually its bright luster.

Holy Father Peter, intercede for us!

2. Father Tom

Unlike some of our other St. John's saints, Father Tom is not exactly a hidden saint. His wake was a two-day party with people coming in from all over, giving performances and talks and meeting one another, and his funeral filled a large east-end church to overflowing. He'd served as pastor of large parishes and spent his life doing long-lasting work with all sorts of people. He was lively and fun, and had a deep, strong mind.

What's more hidden, though, is the life and new ministry he found as Grandfather to the Poor at St. John's Mission, in the last years of his life.

He was retired and living in a downtown infirmary for priests when, by some chance or grace, we met. I knew of him but didn't really know him; that was about to change, to my everlasting gratitude. At that point, his speech was slowed and gait inhibited from the effects of a stroke. But his tall, strong frame was still imposing, his mind still incisive, his heart rich and deep and gracious. And he was restless to be serving. He was a lover of the poor, a lover of the layperson and the young person and the little one, a delighter in joy and beauty and people meeting each other and in sports (un-

official chaplain to the Blue Jays, as his wall photos attested), and social justice, and, well, the Lord. There was only one Father Tom (or Tommy, as he liked to be called) McKillop.

His pastoral side was on the alert from the first moment we talked, and he was eager and ready to help. St. John's Mission at Broadview was, at the time, pretty skeletal as to volunteers — Toronto hadn't yet established its volunteer program for people on social assistance, we weren't officially part of 'Out of the Cold,' and we hadn't been at Broadview long enough to be really part of that neighborhood yet. Fernando's strong, steady presence, a trio of women (blood sisters) who came every Wednesday evening to cook and eat with the neighborhood folks, Peter's prayerfulness, Angela's stalwart service — these were some of the pillars of the Mission then, strong but few. Most importantly, that year, the founder, Father Roberto, was taking his first-ever (and still only) sabbatical, a whole year off the continent and out of touch, which was somewhat heart-stopping for us all. Certainly it was for me, left in charge of the Mission's life and management. And in that vulnerable moment, when all could have collapsed, this tall, broad-shouldered, baseball-playing priest, physically weakened, with an unweakened heart for the underdog and a love of the social Gospel — Father Tom — walked right in and claimed his place.

I loved Father Tom for not 'doing' much, and not worrying about 'doing' much. He was there. He was there from start to finish every day we were open that year, sitting in the refectory, eating, drinking coffee, talking with the folks, listening, listening, not judging, listening, blessing us by his being and his presence and his unshakable, unbreakable conduit to God's love. This was a man who'd walked with the likes of Viktor Frankl and John Howard Griffin. He'd founded Youth Corps, a well-established ministry for youth which served the Toronto area for years. He'd received the Order of Canada. (Not that he talked about any of that.) And now, every day its doors were open, he sat at

St. John's and waited for the most important person in the world — the person off the street — to come in and be welcomed, and met as a human being and child of God.

The people of the Mission, especially the homeless men, loved him right off. So many had lost or become disconnected from their fathers and grandfathers, sons and brothers, not to mention their own fatherhood, and here was a holy, playful, priestly grandfather-Father. He loved them back, without preference or judgement, and treasured his time there.

He also loved the liturgical life, this man who'd served as a Roman Catholic priest for more than thirty years. He was introduced to Orthodox morning and evening prayer, to the Great Canon of St. Andrew of Crete, and to the story of Mary of Egypt. Who could be unmoved by watching him, with great care and suffering, lower his six foot four inch frame to the ground for full prostrations, over and over. He dedicated himself to the Jesus Prayer. He prayed for and carried each person there. He asked if he could be buried with a *chotke* (an Orthodox prayer rope) in his hands.

Many people who would never otherwise have found the Mission came there because Father Tom was there: people of all backgrounds, people who knew him or knew of him, people who simply were drawn by who he was.

Later, Father Tom became more enfeebled, moved to a home with a higher level of care but farther away, and was unable to come to the Mission. Some of us came to him, visiting him at the Houses of Providence where he spent his last years. How could we not? We couldn't live without seeing and visiting him, if we had any choice about it. He never forgot the people who captured his heart, from Dave Stieb (ace pitcher for the Toronto Blue Jays) to Bill, who was a regular at the Mission while Father Tom was. To the end of his 84 years, he wrote poetry about what he'd witnessed and lived.

These things were visible to the eye, and made it tough for any heart in his presence to remain of stone. Less readily evident was his deep prayerfulness. That, perhaps, more than anything, even more than his down-to-earth love of people and of sports, made him the glue that so clearly held the Mission together during that extra-vulnerable year, and the years after when he still could come.

Of all the Father Tom stories I could tell, the one most moving to me happened in the length of time it took to speak one sentence. It changed my heart forever, and gave me a gift without which I

could not have done the work that has since been given to me. I had heard news of a high-ranking cleric who'd made a decision that would have far-reaching negative consequences for St. John's — without consulting or speaking with any of us. Inflamed, I instantly made ready to set out and, in person, give that clergyman a hot piece of my mind. Father Tom saw it coming, and (initially) irked me by putting a hand on my shoulder and asking me to sit down a moment in the office. Even so, I knew enough to obey. He told me, quietly, that I did not know what that person had actually said or done, what he meant to say or do, and that I had better start by listening and praying. I don't know if anybody else in the world, not even my father, could have caught me and altered my path that day. Not only did it have immediate good effect, but it also taught me a way of being and acting that has steadily guided me ever since.

Father Tom was born into this world on January 30, 1928, and left it for eternal life on February 15, 2012, just after his 84th birthday. When I pray to him, I ask him for the grace to listen and rejoice in others, especially the outcast, the old, and the young.

Holy Father Tom, pray for us!

3. Helen

Helen is one whose life in God we really came to understand only after her death.

I happen to have been the last person to see her alive. She'd been in hospital for some time, and when I came in she was alone, breathing painfully. As I stood by her bed, it came over me like a thunderclap that a sign said "Nothing by mouth," but she had no tubes of any kind. I went out to ask a nurse to get the doctor for me, and when I came back a moment later, there was no more breath. When the doctor finally came, he stood silently, looking at her and then at me across her body. "Did you send for me?" he asked. "Yes, I wanted to ask why she is being allowed to die of dehydration, but you see she has died." He said he had just arrived on duty and had never met her before, confirmed her death, and departed. "Out and over," as Helen used to say at the end of every conversation.

Shortly afterward the chaplain came to the door, looked at me, asked if I was okay, and left. Then the nurse came in, gently held the lifeless hands, drew the curtains around us, and prayed for Helen.

Helen was a regular at the Blake Street St. John's from its very beginning. Father Roberto first spotted her bent-over, digging through a flower box at the front of St. John's, looking for pennies. The two of them eyeballed each other. It was like meeting in the garden of the Resurrection. And it was instant love: she never forgot that moment, and she never left the place. She became a fixture, sitting by the door of the Chapel, or sitting on a bench folding laundry (her own special task and place in the community), and welcoming newcomers and familiar faces alike.

When she came to the Mission, she was poor, she was alone. She spoke so softly that you had to bend down near her to hear, and since her speech was somewhat garbled, she sounded like a bird chirping. She was easily overlooked. She craved human companionship, but was unable to articulate her immense pain. We eventually realized that her mind had broken because of her family experiences and from excess of grief. This became clear when she fell and was taken — for the last time, as it turned out — to hospital, and Paul offered to go into her apartment and feed her birds. She lived alone (with the birds) in 'the Blake,' the subsidized apartment block which brought St. John's to Blake Street. The state of her place was clear evidence that she was no longer sane. With the help of Fernando, we spent several excruciating days restoring it to order — which made us feel better, though she herself never saw it again.

At one of our retreats in Collingwood, Pierrette spent time with her, and was able to hear her speak about the horrors of her life, and write her story. We'd wondered, at times, how a woman with ten children could be so alone. That day in Collingwood, Pierrette learned that, little by little, all Helen's children had been taken away by Children's Aid. She heard stories like the day Helen's husband tried to poison their children's school sandwiches by lacing them with rat poison, and that another day, he bent some of her fingers back until they broke. We saw that Helen had simply decided, at some point, the only way to survive was to depart from sanity.

"Hanging in," was her response if you asked her how she was, and that was a pretty accurate description.

The holiness of Helen is not just that she went through horrors and yet somehow retained a purity and sweetness, not even just that she was a living fountain of grief for her children, but that when she came to the Mission, she was instinctively drawn to the Chalice. She would come up for the Chalice and insist on receiving communion. It might have looked as though she was just a poor woman coming to St. John's for distraction and for the community meals. But for her, St. John's was her church; intuitively she believed that this was the Church and she came there because it was the Church. She couldn't put it into words, but she was drawn to the Church and the Eucharist.

To the Church she brought the pain of her life that made her lose her sanity. The long hours she would spend by the doors of the church, just sitting and keeping watch, were her 'place' there, and her teaching for us.

Only after many, many years among us did she trust us enough to show us, one day at Broadview, her feet. Those feet gave her acute pain which she kept to herself as long as she could. When she finally let us sit her down and take off her shoes and socks, the student nurse's mouth dropped open when she beheld Helen's feet.

During liturgy, she held the Gospel Book as though it was Christ himself. At that moment, her place in the community was most exemplified and liturgized, because she was the one who held the Gospel while it was being read. She was the perfect height: she didn't need to bend over, but stood straight with the Book resting on her head. So her littleness gave glory to God because she could hold the Gospel at the right height.

Helen had a keen sense of hospitality; she loved to bake, and would rarely come to the Mission without bringing her latest batch of muffins. Once we'd seen her apartment, we had some idea of what it cost her to bake them. And her true sense of hospitality was revealed in that final hospital stay, during her expedited dying, when she drew the women of the Mission around her. They spontaneously kept vigil with her, becoming in those last days the women at the cross, the myrrh-bearing women.

4. Carol Anne

Often, here in the Church, we say how we are to convert the poor, to evangelize the poor. What I have learned is that the poor also evangelize the Church.

Carol Anne was one of those people who opened my heart to Christ in a way that has deeply marked my life. She suffered from severe mental illness. In one of her lucid moments, she shared with me the story of her first personal encounter with God as a young girl on a boat near Vancouver. In a real way, the hand of God did rest on Carol Anne.

One of those deep exchanges took place one day when I was hiding in the chapel, burdened by many doubts and sorrows. Carol Anne walked into the chapel, went straight to the icon of Christ and began to pray out loud in the empty chapel. She eventually also prayed for me, naming those things that burdened my heart at that moment. On her way out, she turned to me and said: "Father Roberto, remember Christ is risen!" It was July! It reminded me of St. Seraphim's prophecy that they would sing "Christ is Risen" in July. To this day, I can't say or hear "Christ is Risen" without remembering Carol Anne.

Eventually, the illness that was oppressing her mind took her life. She escaped from the hospital where she had been locked up and jumped off the Bloor Street bridge.

Holiness and deep human brokenness, this is the witness of the Church at St. John's.

Also, evangelization is not just a one-way effort. To evangelize, you must also be open to being evangelized by the poor.

5. Edna

In the Scarborough mission, there is a photograph of Edna sitting in the chapel at Broadview, with light streaming down on her. It reveals her deep soul, but her life was anything but peaceful or easy. Edna's history at St. John's was a very long one, one that continued for many years with true friends that carried her until her last breath. Edna left home at 14, preferring the safety of the Toronto streets to her home in the north of Ontario. She could not remember how many times she had been in jail, and learned to drink melted-down vinyl LPs when there was no alcohol. Married to a committed alcoholic, she remained faithful to him till he died.

On one Holy Wednesday, she made a vow in the chapel to stop drinking, and never took another drink for the rest of her life. She had enormous willpower, and an inner life that would sustain her in a hospital bed for months with no food or drink, no TV or video, yet smiling whenever I would visit her.

At the Mission she was always larger than life — loud, generous, she loved to laugh, or start a fight if necessary! There were many sides to this

incredible woman, however one that for me touches the core of her soul took place early on in our friendship on Blake Street. One day, after vespers, I found Edna in the kitchen screaming, with a knife in her hand and wanting to kill herself. Over the next several hours, I learned about her story of sexual abuse and violence. Her body and soul were broken at an early age. Anger, rage and hurt at her present relationship were breaking her heart. After a while, and some silence, I asked her to pray. She refused. After more time passed I asked her again. Again she refused, saying she never prayed — she was United Church, after all! After some more silence she began to pray, "Lord..." I expected words of sorrow, of rage toward others, toward God, but instead she said, "Lord, thank you!" And she listed the names of all the people who had shown her love at the Mission. It was at that moment that I felt that this woman was being taught by the Holy Spirit the exact prayer to say that would heal her wounds. Who else can teach us how to pray?

Edna showed a harshness, it is true, but that concealed a child-like quality that I believe opened heaven to her. I was told that her last words were, "Father! I am sorry." Many people continue to remember Edna, both at the Mission and in our neighborhood.

Holy Mother Edna, pray for us.

6. John

Today, John is the newest presence among the people of the Mission, but when thinking about the holiness of the poor, his name is the first to come to my mind.

Initially, he came to the Mission for breakfast on an early Saturday morning. Coincidentally or not, it was also the day of the birth of St. John the Baptist. John is in his seventies, and he has been homeless for seven years. As he told me, he is not quite sure if this happened by chance, or of his own choice. It is quite obvious that there is nothing poetical about living on the streets. As people tell us, the streets are a world of violence, where the weak and the most vulnerable are stepped upon. Many of those living on the streets struggle with different forms of addiction and mental illnesses. As John says, even if one manages to remain sane and stay away from addictions under such circumstances, it is extremely hard to live a life like that.

'Homed people' like to think that mental illness or addictions lead people to live on the streets. It might be true in some situations, but no matter how sane a person might be, ending up on the street by chance or by choice will wound in different ways. Being homeless is a fight that leaves scars.

In this world of violence, John is looking for peace. On that first morning when we met, he told me about the presence of God in our lives, and how we should focus solely upon this presence. He also told me about his love for Jesus and the work of the Holy Spirit, about the temptations of the flesh — which is weak — and the spirit of God, who will consume our hearts no matter how petrified they might be. He talked about people's misconceptions about hell. The fire of hell, he said, is the love of God, who embraces us but we are not able to come out of ourselves. He told me that the source of evil lies within the selfishness of our being, but in the end, nothing can resist to the love of God.

John knows a lot about religion; he is not churched, but he speaks from his own experiences. When talking about the grace of God and how it works in our lives, he told me a story that happened to him. He was in Scarborough one evening, and some young people, in their twenties, approached him. They intended to hurt him, only because he was different. It was a brutal form of racism. He felt it was very real. He understood they were going to harm him, but he did not react in any way and he said nothing to them. Violence looks for violence, he says. It can only be conquered through peace. After threatening him several times, the youngsters decided to leave him alone, seeing he had no reaction. After they had left, he realized how close he had been to being hurt, or even losing his life. What kept him safe was his composure. But then he added "that did not come from me." You cannot be still when your life is under threat. The fear is too strong. It is impossible not to react. John believed that it was only God's grace that kept him alive in that moment.

The last time I saw John was at the feast of the Dormition of the Theotokos. Before the feast, during the fast, John had seen us decorating the icon of the Theotokos with flowers, in preparation for the Paraclesis service. When he saw the icon, he started to cry, and he told me that he had a special devotion for the Mother of God since his youth. When I came for the Liturgy the next morning, John was lying at the entrance of the church. He had come for breakfast, only to realize that there was no breakfast program that morning because it was a feast day. I told him he could come inside to rest because we had a service. He came inside before seven a.m., and remained in silence for two hours in front of the tomb of the Mother of God. He then stayed for two more hours for the Liturgy, and it was his first time attending an Orthodox liturgy.

John is a true hermit. One who lives on the streets of Toronto. Our first conversation ended with John realizing that he had spoken too much, and he needed to return to silence. Which he did.

I don't know if and how John could live within the church. At the Mission, we see that the Holy Spirit brings people together in church in so many different ways, preparing the place that is personal to them. I don't know what that might be for John. I just have a desire to have him join us more and more for prayer. I am afraid to tell him that, though. I can just wait and hope that his freedom and love for God will bring fruits for all of us at the Mission, right here at 155 Broadview Avenue.

7. Nick

Nick is a miracle in himself. His life and his story would inspire and touch any heart.

Nick has boldness toward goodness, and a special sense of humor. When I went to bless his home, I felt so much peace in his apartment that I did not want to leave. His home was like a living embodiment of the story of the two monks from the *Patericon*. The order and lack of it were reflecting the presence of God. Everything was clean, and out of place.

Nick's life story is a simple one. He was working in a factory for a while, in a place that he really loved, and then he got sick. He developed schizophrenia, a terrible illness that made him lose his job. For many years, as Nick says, every day he felt like killing himself. That is what the voices would tell him. "Do you know how hard it is to fight against those thoughts? It is very hard. You have no idea." That is what Nick would say when he hears other people complain about their own lives.

Something changed in Nick's life when he started learning to play the guitar. He is definitely not one born to be a musician. He never had anything to do with music before he became ill, he just de-

cided one day to learn music by himself and so he did. He started with basic music theory, studying books by himself, without any help, for many hours a day, for many years. Today, Nick can play classical music on his guitar. Only classical music. He ordered books from Europe, and he plays music from the seventeenth, eighteenth and nineteenth centuries. Nick says that playing the guitar saved his life. This is what he most likes to do — even when he comes to the Mission, he plays his guitar for us, and we listen (at least, when the place is not too noisy).

Nick is baptized. He comes to the Liturgy, he comes for confession and he takes Holy Communion. He prays, and he lives his faith in a simple and practical way. Every Wednesday, he comes to our small Bible study group, where we reflect on the Sunday gospel, the way we see it in our lives.

It was on one of these occasions that Nick told us how he ended up coming to the Mission. Nick has all kinds of friends, and he knows many people. Some of them, as he says, have a bad influence on him. It was under such influence that Nick found himself one day fighting with a very dangerous man. Nick has a strong build and he is not one to be easily intimidated. As he got into this fight, he realized that his opponent could seriously harm him or even kill him. He promised God, during the fight, that if he would get out of it alive, he would change his life completely. The fight must have been really serious, because someone called the police. They managed to stop the fight, and arrested Nick's adversary.

A few days later, Nick heard from one of his friends about our bakery, and the possibility of volunteering. He then came to the Mission. He believes that God sent him here, to help him keep the promise he had made during that fight.

He leads a simple life outside the Mission. He earns his living by doing cleaning and landscaping for his building. He gets to stay there for free. Sometimes, he misses Sunday Liturgy because he needs to take care of his father, who lives by himself in a seniors' home. His father is sick and almost blind, so Nick does his father's shopping once a week, and he cleans his apartment. Nick loves his father, but he cannot stand hearing him praise the benefits of communism.

A few months ago, Nick had to choose between his car and his apartment. The financial arithmetic would not allow him to keep both. He decided to give away his car, even though he really loved driving. It was hard for him, but with his witty sense of humor, he later admitted that sleeping in a car wouldn't have been a very good idea.

Recently, Nick told me that he would like to leave Toronto, and asked if I could help him do that. He wants to go to Africa and do missionary work. I tried to convince him that he doesn't need to go that far for that kind of work. We are trying to do the same thing right here, at the Mission. But it might take a bit more to convince Nick, maybe some changes in the way we do things around here. Nick is a very practical man, and when he says something, he means business.

In the meantime, Nick is still struggling with his sickness. He is on medication, and at times it feels like he is losing the battle. Sometimes, e blames his illness for his losing his previous job, and his car, and his former lifestyle. Then he realizes he might have never learned to play the guitar, or stepped inside the Mission, had he remained healthy.

We all look for change in our lives, but Nick is living that change fully. *Metanoia* is real, but not the way we picture it. Rather, *metanoia* is real the way Nick lives it.

8. Anna

I once heard a Romanian monk say that God is so humble that, even when people are told that they missed a chance to encounter Him and do His will, they would still talk back to him. Like they do on the day of the last judgement: when did I not feed you, clothe you or visit you? This can happen, the monk said, because God comes to us in humility. This is something that is strange to us, but not to Anna.

Anna is a simple single mother who is in her seventies, but you would not even say that she is sixty. When I thought about the holiness of the poor, her name came to me at the end. And this is not because I have doubts writing about her. I wrote an article about her for the Mission's newsletter, for the edition dedicated to the holiness of the poor, but somehow I did not send it for publication. It is probably for that same reason: her humility. Anna is so humble that you don't notice her, or, if you do notice her, you know that she will wait for you, and never be offended. (That's what we think about God too: He can wait.)

Anna has the gift of seeing the goodness in people, and she would tell you that in a way that

does not make you feel embarrassed. Anna was born in China, and immigrated to Canada with her husband. They had a really hard life here. They worked morning till evening to make a living, but she never complains about that. As a result of the hard work, her husband died of a heart attack, and left her alone with three children, whom she raised on her own. Now they are all adults, and Anna is taking care of her nephews, anytime they need her. One time, Anna told me how she stayed in the Sick Kids hospital with Benjamin, one of her nephews, who was born with a heart problem and required surgery at an early age. He had to go back periodically, and she was there with him all the time. She always thinks about him, and puts some sweets aside for him when she finds something at the Mission.

One of her sons is still living with her. He has a terrible skin disease, and no medicine can help him, although he has tried everything. He spends most of the time indoors, with no hope to find a job, or anything good for him in this world. But Anna has hope. She never despairs. She prays to God, and thinks only He can help her son (not the medicine alone).

Anna helps peeling vegetables, or anything we need, when she comes to the Mission to eat. She attends all our church services. When we pray at the Mission, even during the long hours of vigil or Sunday Liturgy, she is the first to come into the church, and she prays in silence before the service.

Anna went to a Catholic school when she was young. Her mother sent her there. She says that the life of prayer that we have at the Mission reminds her of that time, when she prayed with the nuns. She said that now, "it is like you can breathe again." And she breathes to show me how she feels. Anna does not read English well, but when she is in church, she learns the words, and with boldness she started to sing with the choir. Over the years, you can hear her voice getting more and more clear.

She told me recently that her great sorrow is that her children are not coming to church. But you know, she says, "I keep praying and praying to God that eventually they will — God can do everything."

One thing I forgot to mention: every time Anna speaks, she is smiling.

We try to keep things simple at the Mission. In humility, Anna lives a simple life. Prayer needs simplicity, where simplicity becomes beautiful through prayer. Just like Anna.

9. Daniel

One could write a book about Daniel. One only needs to listen to him talking and then take record of it. A few good volumes could come out of it.

Daniel is an active person in his community. He knows many people, and he has many friends. He has been blessed to meet some extraordinary people in his life, people with a life of faith and love of God, who have touched his heart. Most of them are also struggling with mental illness.

Daniel lived in a Franciscan community for a few years. Father Joe, a well-known Catholic priest, was close to Daniel in some of the most difficult moments of his life. Daniel recalls an event that happened when he was living in an intentional community. He had to dress up as a clown, and Father Joe told him he had never looked any better. This must have made a strong impression on Daniel, since he still remembers it to this day.

I first met Daniel when he came in for a counselling session. He ended up counselling me. After my ordination as a priest, I tried to bring Daniel closer to the community, so that we could pray more together. I did not necessarily succeed in

doing that, but Daniel would always say a prayer at the end of our counselling sessions, and after that he would give the dismissal, as he likes to say. After a while, I took Daniel to the bakery to help me make the prosphora. He soon decided to volunteer at the bakery every Thursday, helping to make the bread. He was happy to bake, but when his help was not needed for shaping the bread any more, he agreed to do dishes in the bakery, and he did them with the same great joy. Once in a while, he would bring a home-baked treat to share with his friends in the bakery.

Daniel is a poor man living on ODSP (which means he can gain only a limited amount of extra income before having the benefit reduced). However, when we offered to pay him for the hours he worked in the bakery, he said he wanted to feel that he did something out of his own heart and time. But he said it would be nice if the volunteers could receive a fresh loaf of bread at the end of their work. To this day, it is the only reward he receives.

Daniel did not have an easy childhood; on the contrary, he lived through a lot of pain and suffering. He talked openly about his past on a few occasions at the Mission, and when he was invited as a guest speaker for our annual marriage retreat. I will not give details here, but I can say that Daniel has been diagnosed with PTSD, and he knows the mental health system inside out. One thing about his past that he shared with us is his being locked up in a mental health hospital after being falsely diagnosed, when he was still a child. Years later, a psychiatrist corrected that false diagnosis.

Daniel still recalls the overwhelming violence he was subjected to. He remembers the feeling of extreme abandonment he lived when he was tied to a hospital bed so that he could not move. He says that in that moment he prayed to God, saying that he would accept all the suffering if it came from Him, but if it was not from Him he prayed that he would be delivered. After his prayer, even though he was still tied up, he felt a lot of peace in his heart and no need to fight.

Daniel grew up attending a Baptist church, and he discovered his love for Jesus, as he says, during a camp when he was eleven or twelve years old. He also lived in a Franciscan community for a while, and he now goes to a Catholic church on Sundays, as his girlfriend is Catholic. He prays with us at the Mission. We've prayed the psalter together a few times, and he leads our Bible study group on Wednesdays. He lets me say the prayer at the beginning, and then he prays, giving the dismissal at the end.

There are so many things I learned about Daniel during our counselling sessions and in our the Bible study group. He doesn't read books, but he speaks extremely well, in simplicity and with deep meaning, showing a sharp theological intuition. His reflections are always spontaneous — not prepared in advance — regardless of the occasion he is asked to speak, whether it is at our study group, or other presentations at the Mission, or during retreats.

Daniel taught me that we need to have hope, and if we don't have enough hope we should pray to have more. "If you don't have hope for people, you don't have hope for yourself, and if you don't have hope for yourself, you see no hope in people." His girlfriend once asked him why children or anyone else need to suffer. Daniel said to her, "I don't know. If I knew, it would be like I had seen the face of God." During our prayer groups, Daniel urges us to make "prayer couples," meaning to pray for another person during the week, and then he offers to pray for all of us. He tells us how he prays even when he is walking, sometimes aloud, with no concern that people around him might think he is crazy. Or how he used to pray for hours while having a bath, and coming out with his skin looking all funny. He gives us these examples because we need to pray, as he says, unceasingly. This is what he learned from one of his friends when he went to consult with him about one of his problems. "Did you pray about this?" his friend asked. "Yes, I did." "But did you pray about that?" "Yes, I did." "But did you pray about the other thing? What about that, or that, or that...?" "You see," says Daniel, "he was asking me to pray unceasingly."

Daniel also told us about the parable of the mustard seed and its small size. It is not really just about the size, but about the growing. I always feel like I should take more notes of Daniel's reflections, so that I may tell them to people in church, so that they may hear the voice of the poor.

Daniel is also struggling, like all of us. Forgiveness, he says, is the key. He says we don't forgive because we don't let go of the power that we have over the other person. But he forgives by taking care of those who have suffered like him. He attends a PTSD group, and he listens, comforts and supports others who have experienced similar pain to his in their lives.

Daniel is a free spirit, but he believes in love. He believes in marriage. He prayed to God that He would help Daniel meet a person with faith, a person who is "on fire with God." And Daniel did meet such a person, which is why he was invited to be a guest speaker at our annual married couples' retreat. But, that story would be another volume in itself.

10. Karl

Karl is like a rare and beautiful bird. You get to see him every four to six months, if you are lucky. There is so much peace in his heart, that when you meet him you don't want him to leave. It seems that every time he does come, I am either dealing with a crisis situation somewhere, or I am doing a service, or I am late for something. I never get to talk to him for too long, so I know very little about his life. What I do know is that he lives in a subsidized neighborhood, and cares deeply for the people living there.

I remember one time when he was deeply disturbed by a crime that had happened on the floor where he lived. Not only by the crime, but also by the consequences of a violent death that, somehow, he was sensing. He wrote the name of the person who had died in our prayer book, so we can pray for him in church.

Karl is a Catholic and he lives like a hermit, which is why he 'avoids' us. I tried to invite him to different gatherings or groups organized at the Mission. He never refused the invitation, but he never came either. He was born in Canada, but then he moved to the U.S. He was living there with part of his family (he wasn't married), until one day when he suddenly felt that he should go back to Canada. When he told his relatives about his desire, they were perplexed. But that did not deter him from his decision.

He departed for Canada by foot. He walked. He told me, "You cannot believe how people from everywhere helped me on the way." It sounds like Mother Gavrilia's story. When he had no idea how he was going to get any farther, a car would come and another kind person would drive Karl for another stretch of the road. When he finally got to the border, he realized he had no passport. But he ended up on a bus that was crossing to Canada without needing to have his papers checked at the border. (We hear all kind of stories at the Mission every day, but Karl speaks the truth.)

A few years ago, Karl wanted to talk to me. If he does come to the Mission, it would be in the morning, for the breakfast program, around six a.m. He was deeply impressed with the life of a particular saint. He confessed he was fond of St. Francis, but he had read about St. Anthony, and his heart was touched. I took Karl inside the chapel to show him the icon of St. Anthony we have there. We talked about the saint. Karl was really moved. He told me again that his favorite saint was St.

Francis, but he saw St. Anthony as a force, as a pillar.

I know, from talking to Karl, that he prays. I once asked him to pray for me and he answered me, smiling, "I thought you, as a priest, are supposed to do that for me."

Karl is trying to live a life away from today's technological influences. He gave up his TV set, but he has a passion for soccer and his favorite team is Liverpool. When the soccer season starts, his heart weakens again and he gets another TV so he can watch his favorite team play. This is not an easy fight, but he doesn't give up.

Karl proves that life is not about being successful, but about the way you live your own failures.

11. Xenia

Xenia is, as some would say around here, a tough cookie. She does not like sweet talk. She is straightforward, and sometimes abrupt. She knows the Bible inside out, and she always carries a copy in her bag.

I often feel like she can see inside one's heart, at least inside mine, when I talk to her. She demands attention, making sure your thoughts don't stray when she talks to you. She can be blunt, but she seems to expect the same from you. She can sense immediately if communication is not real, and she will not hesitate to tell you so, quite abruptly. There were times when I had unplanned conversations with Xenia, which lasted more than an hour — sitting on the stairs in front of the Mission, for instance.

I would sometimes consciously or unconsciously try to avoid her for the same reason that makes me look for her words. I have met people who could 'see through you' before, but Xenia will also let you know that she can.

One time, she was concerned about a community member who had suffered a stroke. She visited him at the hospital a few times, and when he was discharged she wanted to make sure we were taking good care of him. She came to me a few times with suggestions about how to best care for our dear friend. Although I knew he was being cared for, I also knew there were some discouraging signs about him. She asked me to apply some of her recommendations, and to be more involved in caring for our friend. I promised her I would find out what was going on with him. Later that day, Xenia asked me again if I had any news. When I told her what I found out, Xenia swiftly replied "You know, from my own experience, I realized that it takes much more energy to postpone things than to do them."

Xenia has a strong faith. She reads her Bible daily — some of the pages are starting to tear apart. She prays intensely and she purposely lives according to the Gospel. Xenia has a house that her parents left her, but, as she says, she does not have the means to maintain that house. During winter, the house gets very cold, since she cannot afford heating. So Xenia stays in shelters or with her friends, coming to the Mission early in the morning and sometimes not leaving until late at night. I sometimes see her so tired during wintertime. Many a time, I've found her inside the chapel sitting still, making me wonder whether she was sleeping, or praying, or both.

Xenia has never been married and, as she says, she has never even been kissed on the cheek. She likes to sing and she has a beautiful voice. When she is in good spirits and there is music at the Mission, she will even dance.

Xenia confessed with tears in her eyes that what she experienced at the Mission filled her heart more than all the doctors and the treatments she has had throughout her life. She feels loved and cared for at the Mission. She often mentions how she felt when she was entrusted to play a part in a Shakespeare play at the Mission, directed by Brother Luke. She played the queen, who forgave the husband who killed her. Forgiveness. She said that is the forgiveness of God for men. "That is what I played. I forgive, I forgive, I forgive you!"

Xenia shows deep care for the people of our community, in spite of her bluntness. She takes care of them in her own way. She visited Mike at the hospital, and paid for his phone. She donates the little money she has to the Mission, and she buys knitted articles from Fran to help raise money for the kids' camps. She talks to people and she shows concern for their well-being.

I remember an incident that happened between her and George, a community member who has some anger issues. He can easily lose control and become violent. Some people use anger to fuel all kinds of feelings — he gets crushed by it.

On that particular day, he was on the edge. We could all feel it. But Xenia was constantly picking on him. George told me she had been doing it all morning. I could not understand why she was doing it. She kept poking and poking him like a big bear. That day did not end up well.

Our man threatened to kill a couple of people, including a staff member. And he is not one to use anger in order to obtain things, he is actually used by anger.

I found out later that he had serious issues going on in his life at that time. In spite of the incident that happened between him and Xenia, several months later they were chatting and smiling together, as if nothing had ever happened between them. George came to me, laughing: "Can you believe that?" I might be wrong, but I felt that Xenia had a plan that day. It looked like she was poking him on purpose, like you would poke a balloon to help it lose a little bit of air so it does not break.

There are many things I've heard and learned from Xenia. I could learn even more, had I the courage to sit down and be poked by her. One day, she gave me a lengthy lecture about patience. "Do you know what lies at the root of patience? Suffering. It is suffering. That's why patience is of the Lord."

It is not just what Xenia says that is impressive, but the way she lives. Xenia does speak about her life, without ever giving us the whole story. Some things stay hidden, the parts that would give you her true measure. One thing I do know is that she has battled severe depression, and that she came close to committing suicide.

This was not only her own battle — people in two previous generations of her family had committed suicide. It is hard even to imagine that.

She was 'supposed' to follow the same route, if we believe what the new research says, but she took a different path, and she won the battle through the grace of God.

Last winter was not easy for Xenia. She got sick because of the cold in her own house and in the street. She was so tired of going from shelter to shelter, that one time she broke down in tears, saying, "I pray to God to let me learn how to love.

Now, at my age (she is in her seventies), I just started to see, just a little bit, how much I don't."

12. Edward

We see Edward as a gift for all of us at the Mission. He is there to comfort us, and to show us where the light is coming from. He is also there to show us how to avoid chasing the light away, and to receive it open-heartedly, letting ourselves be embraced by it.

Elder Sophrony (biographer of St. Silouan the Athonite) spoke of how the 'reversed pyramid' works, with Christ at the bottom, holding all humankind above. The same applies to the Mission. It is usual for people to disagree and have arguments in a community.

Raymond, our community president, is a simple man who lends a hand at the Mission in different ways. People of all kinds come through our doors, sometimes some of the most rough, especially early in the morning at the breakfast program. They might not always be polite, patient or good-mannered. Raymond has to deal with a lot of rudeness and evil comments. Most of the time, he is not able to enforce the limits, so he gets stepped on and he is mocked by many.

He keeps it all in, and I never see him lash back at his attackers. He would tell us once in a while

that he could not take it anymore, but it would stop at that.

Until one day, when I saw him picking on Edward, the only person he was not afraid of. The one at the bottom of the local pyramid, who would not pick on anyone else. The evil would not be carried any further, it would stop at him. Edward has a hard time forgiving Raymond, but he deals with it as best as he can.

Edward does not speak when you'd like him to. If he doesn't want to talk, he will not do it, no matter how many questions you throw at him. One could think he is stubborn, since it isn't easy to convince him to do anything he doesn't feel inclined to at a particular time. For instance, he will rarely play the piano for us, in spite of my repeated requests. Last year, we took Edward to St. Mary of Egypt Refuge for a community retreat, along with a few more people from the Mission. One evening, we were all sharing thoughts about the Mission and how it affects our lives in different ways. When Edward's turn came, he did not speak, but played the piano for us instead, in a way I had never heard him before and I didn't even know he could.

Edward is the one who spends the most time at the Mission. I've seen him so many times, coming in early in the morning from breakfast, and leaving late at night after prayer, vigil or confessions were done. He told me several times he would like to spend twenty-four hours a day at the Mission. He has also talked about his desire to move there in the future, when his parents are older. He is twenty-four years old now.

For the time being, Edward does whatever task we entrust him with. He sets the tables, he cleans the basement with his friends under George's supervision, he rings the bell for the service, and he reads the prayers with us when he feels like it. During Mission Vespers, he always prays for the Mission. One day, I found Edward dressed in a cassock in church. He said it belonged to him and he wanted to say the prayer with us in the strana.

Ironically, that same day, somebody had donated a small-size cassock to the Mission which I was able to offer to Edward afterward.

The biggest challenge for Edward is to get a full-time paid job. For now, he works part-time at Mc-Donald's, but he is hoping to get a job at the Mission, so that he would not have to miss Sunday services any more. His aspirations are various. He would like to become either clergy — a priest, deacon or sub-deacon — or work in the bakery, or even be second-in-command after Bob as a volunteer coordinator. He was disappointed to hear that some of these jobs bring only part-time income or none at all.

Being among the most vulnerable at the Mission, what Edward would like best is to become a security officer. "To make peace," as he says. Many times I have felt like Edward needs to be protected when at the Mission. He comes at different times during the day, and he encounters various people. More than once, have I seen Edward get upset or mad because he was being mocked or picked on by others. He said he didn't need help, and that he would deal with them by himself. He did not say how, though. He just mentioned he would call 911.

There were a few times when the people who would pick on Edward and his best friend Gordon did not come to the Mission. I asked Edward jokingly if he had done anything to keep them away. He answered back, smiling, "I have magical powers." He then told me about a time when Gordon felt so hurt by a person that he started to cry.

I don't know if Edward has magical powers, but I do believe that God takes care of the most vulnerable ones in a special way. Edward loves the Mission so much because he shows us all a disarming love. When his best friend Gordon was sick, he would call him and visit him several times a day.

Edward is a gift to us all that we must treasure, nurture and receive properly. It is us who are the fragile ones, and not him.

13. Kenneth

Kenneth is a fisherman from Newfoundland, and he has been sleeping on the streets of Toronto for more than twenty years. I have met Kenneth outside the Mission a few times and once, in a streetcar, the look in his eyes almost gave me a fright.

He inspires respect at the Mission. It is thanks to him that we decided to let people sleep on the carpet at five a.m., when we open for breakfast. He was among the first to do that. After so many years, Kenneth still does not speak to anyone, but his smiles and his strength when he wakes up keep us going.

One day, we asked Kenneth to tell us about his life. We were surprised to learn how well-spoken he was. But we were most shocked about what he told us about his life on the street. The amount of madness, loneliness and violence he is confronted with, coming from people and from the system, seems out of this world.

He told us how he got and how he lost his apartment, how the social services don't recognize him, and how he is banned from most shelters. It made me think about the main character from one of Kafka's novels, *The Trial*, who is judged and condemned to death without reason.

Kenneth is a strong person, but when we don't see him come in early in the morning, especially during winter, we worry that something might have happened to him. One freezing winter morning, Bob voiced our concerns: "I didn't see Kenneth this morning. I hope he survived last night."

Once when I was speaking with Kenneth, he confessed he would like, at the right moment, to go back home to Newfoundland. For now, he lives in Toronto, in the madness of our carelessness.

One cold morning, I saw Kenneth leaving the Mission and yelling, "Hell, here I come!" And he was coming indeed.

14. Three Shooting Stars

Oftentimes, we come across people at the Mission who we don't see again, or if we do see them it's rather rarely. Some of them leave a mark on us — the mark of faith, the mark of life. They are alive amid some of the darkest places you can imagine.

I met Ruth at breakfast early one morning during the Holy Week, before Pascha. She came with one of the regular breakfast people, who plays the piano well. (He had come to Toronto all the way from Nova Scotia. He dresses strangely, and sometimes we need to call an ambulance for him because of an overdose. Other times, he just calls it himself for similar reasons.) Ruth came with him that morning, and she became so much a special presence in the room that others would look for her attention, including myself.

There was something in her life that was lived, for real. I remember how a regular Mission person tried to catch her in his nest, one made up of words, smoke and misleading stories. I've seen him succeed before with people from our community, and even clergy. Ruth listened to him, and her answer really silenced him, but without offending. The life she was living allowed her to do that.

I talked to Ruth for only a little time. She came to me to ask about the icons we have that are painted on the walls. Most of the people at the Mission are not really interested in them, or if they are, they don't speak often of them. I found out that Ruth was in her forties, she used to work as a nurse, and she spoke six languages. She told me that she sees in the icons a lot of sorrow and joy, just like in her life. Then she told me where the sorrow was coming from: she lost her job because of addictions. She was abused, but she managed to keep both of her children, until the children's aid society took them from her. She could not fight for them in court, as she had to go back to India to take care of her father, who was dying.

I listened to Ruth and I saw the sorrow and pain. She did not say anything about the joy. I realized later that the joy was coming from her heart, a heart that is struggling with all kind of things, but one that makes a lot of room for God's love.

The second and last time I saw Ruth was on a Saturday morning for breakfast, the first Saturday we decided to extend the breakfast program. She was with her boyfriend. She was in pain, as somebody had punched her during the night and broken her tooth. She was crying from the pain. Eventually, her boyfriend decided to take her to the hospital. I hope to see Ruth again. Her friend still comes to the Mission for breakfast but now, he told me he has a new girlfriend, who is actually much younger.

—

People usually come to the Mission alone. And we meet here. William and Jane came together. They are in their sixties, I think, and they are married. Jane was married before, and she also had children. She was born in a Jewish family, but she chose later on to become a Christian. William never laid an eye on anybody. He was alone all his life before meeting Jane, so lonely that he would speak only with God, he says, nobody else. William is tall and looks strong, but he has a lot of kindness in his eyes, and he cares deeply for those who are vulnerable. Both of them lead a simple life, looking to do the will of God in everything.

They were coming to the Mission for meals, and then stayed for prayer. Jane also became a hearer. They mostly stopped coming when William became really sick. He got cancer of his throat. They did come to the Mission a few times after that, and I saw how transfigured his face was. They asked us to pray for them, and especially for John. I believe it is also our fault that we don't know how to care for people in moments like that.

I met Jane and William again after more than a year. They came back and told us that John was doing well. He had gone through surgery, and the doctors had been sure he was going to die, but then he recovered. William thought the same. "I saw death with my own eyes but I was not afraid. I kept praying. If that's what God wants..." They believe it was a miracle that happened, because of all the people who prayed for them. The doctors could not believe his recovery, and Jane says they use his case as a study in their medical books. But, William and Jane know that was God answering prayers.

I saw William and Jane at the Mission a few weeks ago. They came for lunch, and then asked me to pray for William and his continued health. The last test showed that he was perfectly healthy. They are happy. We prayed in the chapel together. After that, Jane said she really loves the Mission and church here. She thinks that God visits many churches, but he lives here. William told me that when I pray, I have to use words not like they would come from a man, but from God. "You have to stop seeing God through the eyes of people, and start seeing people through the eyes of God." As we were talking, William noticed the icon of St. Herman of Alaska and asked me about him — who he was, and what life he had. I left the chapel and printed a description of the life of the saint. He received the pages, and promised to come back and tell me what he thinks about the saint's life.

I am still waiting for them to come back. We might, or might not, see them again in six months.

15. Chris and Laura

Chris came to the Mission for breakfast one March morning, and afterward he said he wanted to talk to a priest.

And he did. About his addictions, his illness — he is on ODSP — his love for his girlfriend, Laura, who is baptized Orthodox, and who wants to break up with him.

It often happens that people from the Mission confess to a priest, even though they do not come to church regularly, but for Chris it was different. All of us want to change things in our life (more or less). Chris was ready to change his life in a way that would be pleasing to God. He did not have dreams about getting a new job, or about leaving his rooming house to get a better place to live. No, he wanted to marry his girlfriend, to fight his addictions, to pray, to start coming to services, and to follow the lives of the saints.

As he was talking, he took from his pocket an icon he had received from his girlfriend. It was the icon of the Forty Martyrs of Sebastia. I was touched deeply, and I told him that we had celebrated their feast just the day before. I shared with him their story, and what they mean to me personally —

they have a special place in my family as well. Chris left with a promise he would come back for services. He did come a few times. Once, during Great Lent, he stayed for the Presanctified Liturgy as well.

I see Chris every now and then. Sometimes he comes and asks for prayer, or he just comes to eat. He's told me he was growing a small garden at the place he lives, about the herbs he planted and how he takes care of them. One day, he came with his girlfriend. They were back together. She lives in shelters, and that morning she needed two things: some clothes (her belongings had been stolen from the shelter where she stayed), and to come to confession.

I have met people on the edge of committing suicide. I have seen their eyes, and their honesty. Laura had already tried — she had jumped in front of a subway train. Somehow, she had escaped, but her leg had been wounded pretty badly. You can tell by her limping how serious that was. Laura's eyes see through you, and ask for forgiveness, and let you know she forgives you too. Now she is fully alive and she hopes to have children.

I don't know what is going to happen with Chris and Laura. One could not imagine the things that they are going through. But in their hearts, they are pursuing goodness and bring all their pain to God.

We like to think that the saints are special people with special gifts. I see the holiness of the poor as broken pieces of light, who come apart from our own sinfulness. Laura was wounded by the subway but also by our own sins, the ones we people share together. She is wounded, but amid all the madness she has had to cope with, she is looking for life, and she breathes.

They are learning to breathe together, Laura and Chris.

16. Charles

C harles is a native from the Canadian North. He's from a community that sees snow more often than anything else. Smiling, he told me that you can still enjoy it there in July. But he never complains about that. There are many other things he does not complain about. Like being in the residential school, or being on the streets.

As I write these words, he is about to be evicted from the room he rents, because the owner wants to sell the place. This is a result of our neighborhood getting more expensive and our city prospering — his room is now worth double the money, while his social assistance amount stays the same. He does not complain, and he does not worry about it. He's been homeless before, as he says smiling.

Charles told me many things about his life back home, in the northern territories. He told me how he used to go hunting with his parents when he was young. How he won a contest of harpoon hunting. And how the life of the community changed over time. "You know," he says, "people don't know, and newspapers never wrote about this, but when they forced us to change our lifestyle, to become civilized, in order to make us stop hunting and fishing, they killed all our dogs. The ones we were using for transportation. With the sleds." Seeing my reaction of disbelief, he said firmly, "Yes. All of them. So we cannot go hunting."

Again, he said that to me without complaining. Like a fact. Like other facts from his old community: how people are getting alcohol without having a special store for that, and how drugs infested their community and took over. And how his life was affected by that, too.

However, Charles does not complain because he has forgiven the wrongdoing from his life, and the people who caused him pain. Directly or indirectly.

The first time I heard about Charles was during a sermon by Father Roberto. When Father talked to us, he spoke of a story from many years back, about a person (Charles) who shared with him how he managed to forgive people from his life. Remembering all the trespasses done to him, and how for every one of them he said an "Our Father," for an entire night. He did not stop before mentioning within the Our Father prayer every person who needed to be forgiven from his life. Nobody told him to do that. He did it himself because he felt the hate he was bearing was destroying his soul.

In our tradition, we say many times that the passions of the soul are good energies, designed to help us achieve goodness and to look for the face of God. So anger should not be destructive (it becomes like that through sin), but should move you to achieve goodness. Charles used it this way to get away from drugs. He said, "I got angry with myself. You know, very angry with what I had become at the time." And that helped him stop.

Charles told me later, in a different context, that this happened when he had a vision in church back home. (I know, we often hear that at the Mission.) I don't know what Charles's experience was exactly, but two things made me think seriously about what he said. The first one was that he said he saw back in his vision the most beautiful smile in the world. The second one was about his getting angry with himself before winning the battle with drugs. He never went back to them.

I talked many times with Charles about prayer. He does not understand why people need special accommodation for that. "I just pray like that," and he lets his arms hang down his body to show me. "Sometimes I pray when I stay at the table in silence. People should not know about this. You just pray." He prays when he walks on the street. And he walks a lot. He was confessing that he walks at night and prays, and he gets fed up with all the violence and wrongdoings in the city. He thinks Toronto is a city where people experience the most pain. Sometimes he is really disturbed because of the wrongdoings in the city he can sense and see at night. He said "I feel how all this negative energy gets to me. It is almost like it's getting in my body. And I get angry against all the things I can see and sense."

I tried many times to get Charles to pray with us. I did not really succeed. He came a few times, always curious, but still believing that you do not need special accommodation to pray. He does pray in silence when he eats with us, and I am sure he keeps us all in his prayers.

Charles went through a lot of heavy things in his life. All his culture was taken away from him. Some of us might get upset if we don't get to eat our favorite bread every week, or every day. Charles lost all his culture, his community life, everything that shaped his existence, but, through prayer he made peace with and forgave everyone.

His battle is still ongoing. He talks at times about that. But he is a strong spirit, with a dignity that reveals to us what people can be if forgiveness and prayer are not mistaken for an idle tale.

17. Manuel

Manuel is a fragile soul. At times I fear that we might find out from the papers that he has departed this world. He is homeless, but in a way that not many experience in Toronto. He asks for money on the streets, and he knows what it means to be alone, rejected by people. A human life, disregarded by others.

He asks for money, and he gets extremely angry when people look away from him as he walks between cars at traffic lights. He is not upset because they do not give him money, but because they turn their faces away from him. "What are you going to see on the other side of the street or up in the sky?" he asks. Last Christmas was the worst time. People used to be more generous around the time of the holidays. It was not so that year. Everyone seemed angry and rushing, with no time and nothing to give.

One of the most difficult times for Manuel was when his friend died of an overdose. Manuel did not even know if this person was really his friend, but Manuel was the only person he would talk to at times. Manuel showed me a video he took of the place where he used to ask for money, together with his friend. And he posted it on Facebook. One of its scenes clearly reflects the loneliness he experiences: walking alone on the streets, he asks Google if God exists. Manuel was not joking or wasting his own time, it was a real question for him. Google was diplomatic, replying with "According to . . ." Google was probably trying to avoid any possibility of being taken to court for any illegal beliefs. But somehow, whatever that answer was, it helped Manuel carry on for one more day. One day at a time means something else for him.

Manuel goes through some of the most surreal situations. For instance, he was registered in a housing program meant to assist people who had been convicted in the past. When the program's officials were about to give him the keys to the apartment, they found out his criminal record was actually clear, so he wasn't deemed to qualify for the program anymore. He ended up on the streets again. Another time, as he was again about to receive the keys to a place where he could stay, but the housing department notified him he had to pay an old debt of $500 before he could get into his new place. Unable to pay the debt, he was again disqualified from the program. It's well-known in Toronto that it might take up to ten years before one can get a subsidized room. For Manuel it took a single mouse-click to lose one. To prevent that happening again, he arranged payments to be made from ODSP (government social assistance), in the amount of $50 a month, so the system would have some mercy on him.

One of the best places for him to park himself over the winter was somewhere in the York University buildings, a place where students can go to study at night. He stayed there an entire winter. The following year he tried to help another homeless person, who got him in trouble so he was caught himself, and evacuated.

Manuel has a beautiful smile and a type of honesty that comes from a soul that has nothing to lose.

He knows that his lifestyle is like a circle, and he tries to break out of it. At times he works at the Mission, cleaning the washroom and the chapel, and watering the flowers. Everything he does is done well. Everything he touches when he cleans reflects a little bit of his purity of heart. He talks about his struggles: getting angry being on the street or in the TTC (the public transit system), losing control. But then, he realizes people have not been at fault, and he apologizes. He tries to understand how people deal with their temptations, and how these temptations look when described to a priest. He wants to be prepared to fight them better.

His body shows the signs of a life in deep pain, mostly caused by others. But his eyes take you to a place where there is light in abundance. That's because he does not hide, and because by being humiliated so much, he still has a special sense of humor and self-irony, which are extremely rare these days. One can talk to him only in honesty. He does not hide, therefore you are compelled to do the same.

Manuel comes to the chapel not only to clean it, but for prayer as well, if he does not feel unwelcome. One day, while reading from the Psalms, he confessed that he was not able to submerge himself totally in prayer. He read the prayer, but his heart was not quite present there. I was ashamed to tell him that most of us didn't even realize that. I told him it was normal for somebody who reads from the Psalms for the first time.

Manuel is living his life in a real desert. He is harmed by the heat, the cold, the rain and the snow, but most of all by the absence of people. But through this he has learned the importance of silence. When he does end up in a shelter, he goes there only very late so he does not have to listen to all the negativity that people spread around. "I don't understand why you have to complain about everything — weather, food, shelter, people. I can't really take it anymore."

Now he is somehow trying to connect with our broken community. In the past he told me that when he comes to the Mission early in the morning, he feels this is the only home for him. I was shocked at that time because I would only see him for a few hours in the morning every now and then. Now he spends more time with us, cleaning, talking, praying, and even sometimes reading with us from the Gospel and reflecting on his life. When reading with him the parable of the poor man Lazarus, the Gospel did not need any interpretations. Not to justify his life through that, but just to see its real meaning for us.

I am sure that Manuel is really looking for a home. Many times, when people say they like the Mission and want to spend more time with us, I fear that they might not be ready to commit. With him, it is the other way around. I feel we are not ready for him and ready to commit to him, and we need to repent more, before he could make a permanent house out of the Mission.

18. Gillian and Carlos

Gillian and Carlos did not know each other at first (one comes on Wednesdays, the other on Thursdays) but bring something similar to our community. They resemble each other not only through the common diagnosis society has put on them, but mostly through immense gratitude for being alive, and smiles that never perish.

Even the pain of a loss cannot take that away. Carlos has been here for a lifetime, one of the oldest volunteers we have. He can hardly dislike anything. For instance, he likes the weather and everything it brings. Whenever I ask him how he likes the cold, heat, rain, snow, or anything else that comes with that, his answer is always the same: "I love it," and he means it. He answers with passion. He always prays with us on Wednesdays for Mission vespers, and always for St. John's community. When we went together to a retreat at St. Mary's Refuge together with other people, Carlos wanted to make an announcement. He told us all that "he was happy to be alive and to be among us all." That moment remained within the Mission, like a building stone on which we rely when we get tired of too many failures. At times, Carlos gets really sad because he lost his father years ago. Sometimes he cries out of pain and love for his father, and he needs a hug to help him calm down. He has made many friends at the Mission. He always likes a good joke and he likes to dress up, paying particular attention to hats. He likes to feast, and a few times a year he'll make us gifts.

Gillian is new within our community. She has only been with us for a couple of months at the most. I really hope that she will be with us for the long term. She comes to the Mission through a program for disabled people. She lives in a shelter for women and comes with a support worker, who changes every couple of weeks. She likes sweets like nobody else. And she is always smiling.

Lately, I talked more about her to one of the support workers. I found out that Gillian lived all her life with her parents, who died recently. And she found herself in a shelter, with nobody else available to take care of her. I also found out that there is something she likes more than sweets, and that is the church and praying.

Every Sunday, she is taken to a different church, I suppose depending on the particular worker's preference. She never objects, and she prays wherever she is taken. And all the people from those churches love her. I can really see why.

Prayer makes her happy, and people see that and want to try it too. I did not want to get in competition with other churches, but I did tell her worker that she could come here on Sundays too, because she is known already to our community. She has formed relationships with us, and it would make more sense for her. However, this has not happened yet. Who knows if it ever will? We have learned here to live with what God gives us or takes away from us. And to pray a little bit like Gillian, just to remind ourselves that joy is the anchor of life.

Both Carlos and Gillian are precious gifts for us. They teach us that prayer is really the breath of life, and that gratitude for being alive is what keeps a person sane. Why is there is no bitterness in their lives? Why can prayer make them happy? Why are people like them not even allowed to be born in our country nowadays, since they teach us where the roots of true joy really lie?

I came to realize that what is evil does not get to Carlos and Gillian. Many times, on Wednesday afternoons, we have people who stop us from praying. In all kinds of ways. Some even do that purposely and with bad intentions. There is one such person who tried one day to undermine our preparation for Mission vespers. He often succeeds in spreading a sense of heaviness in the room, and giving people headaches. That day, he was talking loudly and being malicious while we were repeating some chants together. He could not get to Carlos though. After several attempts, the would-be disruptor eventually left the room. Because Carlos continued to sing. And so did others with him.

We gather around Carlos and Gillian, around the most vulnerable ones, because that's how a broken community that breathes life is going to survive.

ST. JOHN
The COMPASSIONATE

ST. SILOUAN
The ATHONITE

Afterword

Jean Vanier's talk at
St. John the Compassionate Mission's Annual
Donors' Dinner, 17 June 2008

T his is holy ground . . . where God resides . . . people with needs come here. Jesus said: when you give a meal, don't invite family, friends — invite the poor. Don't remain in the clan where we tend to flatter each other; don't close up in a clan — open up . . . to those who are pushed aside — then you will be blessed (Luke 14). At the table, we meet each other.

You help people find jobs, get work, and that's good. But there's something deeper needed in the human heart: community, family. St. John's Mission is creating community: to appreciate one another, to love one another. It's not just doing things for people, but to reveal to them that they are special, they are beautiful — because the marginalized have become lonely. Our society is a competitive society. We want to be the best, strong, powerful, efficient. In a culture of competition, some win, many lose, many more are victims. A culture of competition becomes quickly a culture of depression — that's what we're becoming — a culture of depression, and a culture of anguish. People feel lonely, unwanted, pushed aside, and loneliness gives rise to anguish, to the sense that I'm nobody, I'm no good, nobody can care for me — an inner pain, a throbbing pain. This quickly becomes either a place of violence or a place where people need the experience of forgetting, which leads to drugs.

St. John's is a place where people gradually come out from loneliness. But it's not easy. The anguish of loneliness gives rise to violence, to suicide, to drugs. It's too awful, so they go into another world. Sometimes to help this, people move out of the drugs, they go back to loneliness and back to drugs again.

This is the vision of St. John the Compassionate. Compassion isn't just doing things for people, it's revealing to people: you're beautiful, you're a child of God, you have value. Their anger isn't just against society — our competitive society — but the greatest pain is when people become angry with themselves, and begin to hate themselves. This is one of the greatest pains.

How to move from a society of competition to a society of welcome? Is it possible? People accepted as they are? At the heart of the Mission is a deep belief that every person is important. Gangs — a complex question — when you're very lonely you can get into a gang, it gives security, it gives a being with others.

We're in a complex world. The belief here at the Mission is the belief that each one is important, whatever their situation. A community can't take in everybody but it can become a sign, a sign that in this broken city there's a place where people believe that love is possible. Love, not just as an effective reality. For example, there was a leader of the L'Arche community, who was formerly caught up in prostitution. In Sydney, she was walking in the park, and she took in her arms a man who was dying of overdose. His last words were: "You've always wanted to change me. You've never accepted me as I am." Of course we want to help people change, but first they have to discover something — that somebody loves me, that I'm precious. Compassion isn't first of all doing, changing, though we must do what we can for people. First of all, it's the way we look at them, accept them, listen to their story, accept them in their extreme brokenness, and as they discover they are someone, maybe they can begin to change — as we reveal, You're important.

I see many similarities between St. John's and the communities of L'Arche. We have the privilege of welcoming people, people like Patrick, people who weren't able to go to school or find jobs, a lot of pain — in a world of competition, based on the value of winning, people are pushed aside — not having value. It was the pain of people like that. The important thing for Patrick is to know that he's loved — not because he's working in the bakery — you discover that you're precious and then you start doing things.

Jeannine came to our community at 40. She had epilepsy, and hemiplegia (one leg and one arm paralyzed). She quickly manifested much violence, not hitting people, but violent in words, breaking things. In our community, if somebody's violent you should try to stop them; but the essential thing is to try to understand, to help people to verbalize. Jeannie listens to people at St. John's, so they can tell their story, tell their anger, without people telling them what to do, but so they can hear: I understand. Jeannine was angry with her own body; angry because when her mother died she was "placed," "put" in our community, she hadn't chosen it; angry with God because she couldn't have children of her own. It's important to say, "I understand — I'd be angry too" — it's normal to be angry, to be violent. Can we do something about this? How can we help? This can take many years, there's too much pain, it takes time. Jeannine was able to choose another home and that was important to her. Many people with disabilities have been told what to do but not asked their desires. She knew she was being listened to. She didn't like working in our workshops, she worked but it didn't give her life. Singing gave her life, and she loved to dance. As she sang and danced she began to discover she was someone, she had a place. Later, her anger came back: her legs couldn't support her body any longer, and she needed a wheelchair. Becoming dependent made her angry. That's normal. Let's talk about it. Losing her independence made her angry, but then she discovered that as you get weaker you're obliged to say, "I need you." That's the heart of community — that's where community is being born, that's where church is being born, that's where peace is being born. We need each other. When we say "I need you," that helps the other person to find love, to leave the clan, to open up, to discover we can give life to each other.

There are lots of similarities between L'Arche and St. John's. We want to love each other. We need help. As people are called forth to give help, they give life too. I've been in my community now 44 years. I take all my meals there.

The greatest desire of a human being is peace. The greatest fear of humans is war, conflict. I lived through the war of 1939-1945. Two things happened: the discovery of Auschwitz, and Hiroshima/Nagasaki. Today so many people live in situations of conflict, 40 million are refugees. Peace can only come as we start coming out of our ghettos. I was once in Serbia, in the north where there are Hungarians, with a Faith and Light community, in a village that was half Serbian Orthodox and half Hungarian Catholic. I realized the Serbian Orthodox had their schools, their churches, their banks, their groceries, and the Hungarian Catholics had their schools, their churches, their banks, their groceries. I said: "Do you meet each other?" Is that peace? They're not speaking. Yet you're my brother, my sister. We are all of this incredibly beautiful human race. Peace is not the absence of war. Peace is breaking through the barriers that separate groups. Peace is meeting. Tell me your story. I'll tell you about mine. Your vision doesn't put mine in danger. We belong to the same human race.

The community of St. John's is a model, a sign, a sign of peace, in a world where many are locked up in their own little gang. As the price of petrol moves up, we begin to realize we're part of a human family; the prices are rising because we're all interconnected.

I rejoice that Father Roberto invited me here, that I could be with you, to see this community of peace, loving each other, giving 2,500 meals a month as your questionnaire says. And I thank you for being. In our communities, we're terribly fragile. A community like this is fragile. As soon as we're just people, we're fragile. Our communities aren't made of cement, they're made of human, beautiful hearts, that have been broken and are on the way to healing.

ST. MOSES   THE AFRICAN

Illustration sources

Front cover artwork: "Modern Saint In An Urban Desert," by Din. Pencil on paper, 2017.

Illustrations on page 7 (Christabel Anderson, bird), pages 16, 25, 44, 125 and 133 (Andrew Gould, Orthodox cross), and pages iii, 1, 17, 26, 27 and 45: courtesy of the Orthodox Arts Journal, orthodoxartsjournal.org.

Photographs of icons and artwork of St. John the Compassionate Mission in Toronto, on pages vi, viii, 2, 18, 28, 46, 66, 126, 134, 137 and the back cover, and portrait photographs in the "Flowers From the Hedges" chapter: Angela Cass.